HERBS GROW in ❖ the DESERT Southwest

by Charlie Humme

❖

book design & illustrations by Mary Bayless

ACKNOWLEDGMENT

To everyone who has ever touched the
Arizona Herb Association,
To everyone who has ever asked me
a question about herbs and then
stayed around for the answer,
and especially

❖

To Gypsy
I owe tremendous debts of gratitude.

❖

If you think it'll help,
brief portions of this book
may be copied and used
without permission.
Spell my name right.

The reasonable man adapts to society. The unreasonable man expects society to adapt to him. Therefore, all progress depends on the unreasonable man.

George Bernard Shaw

CONTENTS

I value your opinions
Please share your criticisms with me.
FRESH TOUCH GARDENS PRESS
8515 West Planada Lane
Peoria, Arizona 85382

ISBN Title Number 0-9643451-0-2

Book design and illustrations
B² Creative Consultants
P.O. Box 34952
Phoenix, AZ 85067-4952
(602) 254-7220

The best thing a gardener can put on his garden is his shadow.
Unknown

INTRODUCTION

If you live in the desert and successfully grow herbs, DON'T BUY THIS BOOK! At least, not for yourself.

The middle 1980s were significant for more than the crumbling of the Berlin Wall. Like flipping a switch an incredible resurgence in the interest in herbs occurred. Beforehand, herbs were the realm of folks who were interested in pharmaceuticals, ethnobotany, history, magic or religion. Oh yes, a few folks knew you could cook with them. Herbs were low key, though. There were few varieties offered in the seed catalogs. Attempting to purchase herb plants at a nursery was an exercise in folly.

Sure there were pockets of interest in some portions of the country. But the general populace knew herbs only as that which shook out of a red and white box into the spaghetti sauce.

The reasons for the heightened interest in herbs aren't as important to this writing as the interest itself.

The interest increased quicker than the commercial supply so gardeners began to grow their own herbs. How many of us knew, back in 19 and 83, that there are about 30 kinds of basil. You still can get only 'basil comma generic' in the grocery.

It was a wondrous thing that so many folks were cultivating both the herbs and the curiosity. There was trouble in paradise, though. These plants, the bulk of which were originally from Mediterranean climates, were found to be stinkers to grow in the desert. When once asked at the farmers' market, by a nice lady, why she couldn't grow herbs at her home, I was at a loss for words. I think my answer went something like "Ma'am, if everyone could do it, I couldn't make a living." It isn't what I wanted to say, really, but how does one condense his years of mistakes and killed plants, experience and eventual education into a simple conversation at an herb stand in downtown Phoenix?

I think maybe this small book is one way. We in the Arizona Herb Association have helped so many herb growers, both members and not, that we have stopped hearing new questions and are now rehashing the old ones. Therefore, most of the problems have been unearthed and perhaps can be addressed here. That will be what I attempt to accomplish. There is actually more information in here than you absolutely need to do a good job growing. It may not be worded in a way that a pure academic would appreciate. Thus, I hope it is easier to understand. I'm a firm believer that a few extra data might help you 'think out' a problem unaided. You'll get that warm, fuzzy feeling and my phone won't ring off the hook. Naturally, I hope that you also consult other sources of desert gardening information. One under utilized source of help is the Master Gardener office at the University of Arizona/Maricopa County Agricultural Extension. There are some very patient and knowledgeable folks who truly like their jobs of helping the home gardener. ❖

PREFACE

Bad vibrations filled the room. Frustration bordering on anger. My friend's tight jaws were a dead giveaway. "What did I do wrong? I followed the directions in the book exactly. I planted when it said to. I watered the way it suggested. And, yet, look at these dead herbs! I guess I just have a brown thumb."

"The book?" I queried. " Where was the book written?"

"Well, the author lives in Pennsylvania, I suppose it was written there." Herb gardening in the desert is a major frustration when you're transplanted from another climate. Spring in the torrid Southwest U.S. is like Summer anywhere else and Summer is not like anywhere else at all. That which is underfoot in the garden is not like soil as you may have known where you were from. Even our water is not like the water in most of the country. Welcome to our desert.

There are probably hundreds of books on the subject of herbs. Each, no doubt, is the product of someone's experiences and successes. Also, each may have several chapters about the wonders of herbs. Indeed, herbs are wondrous plants and their uses are steeped in history. As medicines they fought our forebear's diseases. They contributed mightily to the gracious living which our predecessors enjoyed. Herbs dyed their cloth, decorated their homes, embellished their landscape designs, and performed countless other uses the memories of which succeeding generations have let slip away.

These herb books admirably describe these marvelous herbs of yore. But when you get to the chapter on how to grow herbs you should skip to the next chapter because not even one has divulged the secrets of successful herb culture in the desert.

The desert herb gardener needs to be part geologist, part chemist, part botanist, part plant pathologist, part horticulturist and part meteorologist. He/She needs to be a purchasing expert and a naturalist. It couldn't hurt if a little entomologist were thrown in for good measure. We need to pay close attention to the things we observe and to evaluate these observations with a conservative eye and not jump to confusions.

No, Toto, we're not in Kansas anymore. It's not too difficult, mostly just different.

I need to tell you something about myself before we go further. I admit I am a hippie retread. I began organic gardening back when such a thing was laughable in the eyes of academe and of agriculture. And long, long before some politician decided that such a thing should be "certified." My schooling and experiences have taught me to observe and to interpret nature as an ally to be cooperated with not as a foe to be conquered. I have noted that it is greed and misunderstanding that have caused our country to develop the incredible array of chemical assaults which has ultimately ruined our aquifers and rivers, squandered our soils, infiltrated our bodies and tainted our food.

I try not to use the word "chemicals" to mean the generic evil. Everything is made of chemicals; you and I and everything you can touch are chemicals combined in some particular matrix.

Many synthetic chemicals are good and useful servants. Many of the chemicals which have caused problems have done so because of misapplication or over application. Had they been used in moderation, we wouldn't be in the fix we're in today.

You ought to know here also, at the outset, that I despise synthetic insecticides and that I don't much like man made fertilizers. I try not to preach, but I wanted to be aboveboard with you, gentle reader. ❖

CHAPTER ONE
Why Grow Herbs?

The reasons that I began to grow herbs as a alternate agricultural endeavor center around a respect for our planet. Herbs use less water than most other crops. Herbs require less fertility than other crops. To my knowledge, there are no synthetic insecticides certified for use on herbs. Herbs are, as we were wont to say in the sixties, sincere. Herb culture is strenuous and intensive and meticulous work which doesn't lend itself well to the modern megafarm. It's a good way to return to the family farm.

There are lots of other reasons a body might like to grow herbs. Many folks have been advised to eliminate salt from their diets. Herbs add flavor. They are beautiful plants, offering wonderful colors, textures, and character to our gardens. Herbs help folks create happiness for themselves and others. Even people not blessed with the gift of sight can appreciate them. The velvet softness of lambs ears, the scents and flavors offer too many examples to list. History buffs can create period gardens of their favorite eras. Theme gardens of all descriptions can be created and in all of these, herbs will play important roles.

We can talk of all these things and more but first let us learn how to grow these temperate plants in our severe environment. ❖

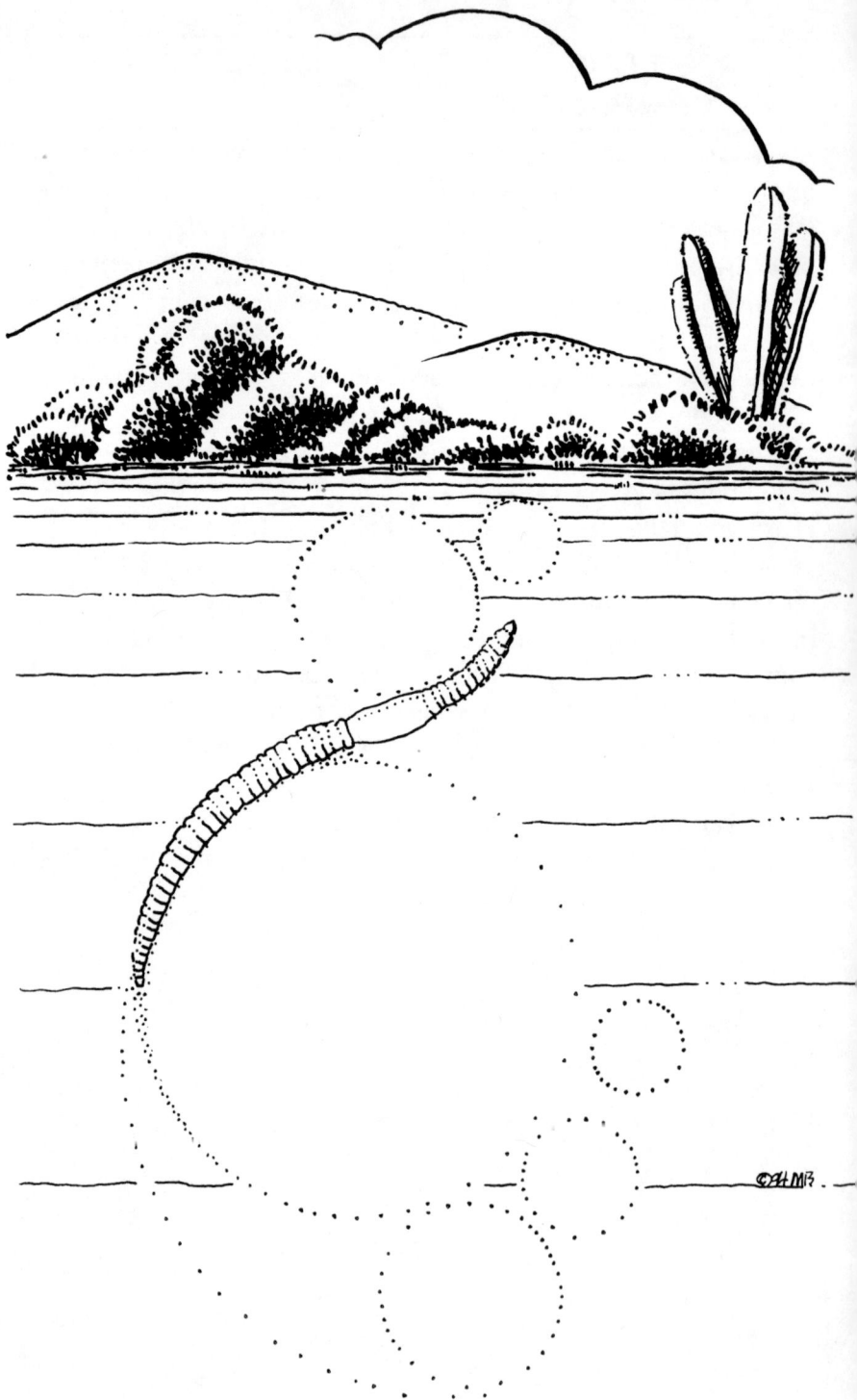

CHAPTER TWO
Soil

There are some herbs which will never grow outdoors in the desert. More specifically, they will never persist throughout the entire year just as there are houseplants for ornament that wouldn't live outdoors. As Dirty Harry said "a plant's gotta know its limitations." On the other hand, some people will attack this problem in the same manner as a deranged governmental agency; they'll throw money at it. Enough shade cloth and mist system might overcome much of the heat and dryness of a summer in Phoenix. But you can't beat Mother Nature forever. Let us accept the fact that growing some plants here pushes the gardener deep into the realm of diminishing returns.

However, many herbs will grow very well here if they are able to establish a proper root system before conditions become too strenuous. A vigorous root system depends on a friendly root environment as well as sufficient time for root growth.

Planting at the proper time in the proper soil are the keys.

Good soil can be built from all but the worst of the desert floor. Yes it can!

Our desert's soils main problems stem from their clayey and alkaline aspects.

The degree of acidity of anything is measured on a system called the pH scale. On the pH scale zero is the most acid and 14 is the most basic or alkaline; seven is neutral. Most herbs like a soil which measures 6.5 to 7.5. Most of our soils are about pH 8. When the soil is that basic, a few things happen which are deleterious to plant growth.

In addition to its basic properties, our soils tend to be composed of a disproportionate amount of the smallest particles, the clay particles. In an alkaline environment, clay particles and the calcium in our water collaborate, tend to form caliche layers which in extreme instances can be several feet thick. In an acid environment, clay particles tend to clump together to form little spheres. Of course, surrounding the spheres will be tiny pore spaces. Imagine a jar full of marbles. Note the spaces between the marbles. If the clay and the calcium form bands they will exclude air and water. Have you ever ground your own coffee and gotten the grind too fine, like espresso? Remember how slowly the water percolated through? You get the idea. No pore space, no percolation of water, no infusion of air and no root growth.

Basic condition has another bad side effect. Some of the nutrients get tied up in compounds which are insoluble. Consider the water stains we all encounter in our sinks. Washing with water (which is rather alkaline) does little to remove them but washing with vinegar (which is an acid) causes them to become soluble and disappear.

So it is in the soil. If we can cause the soil to become a little more acid, we can simultaneously improve its porosity and the availability (solubility) of the nutrients it contains.

Don't be tempted to think that ridding the soil of all its clay is entirely a good thing either. It is a necessary component. More on that point later.

There are pockets of genuinely loose and well draining soils occasionally in our desert. Your garden just might be on top of one of these. Soils change textures all around the country. The nonorganic components of soil are the various Sands, Silt and Clay.

The U.S.D.A. has developed a system to classify soils according to the percentage of each in any given sample of soil.

Their classification is often depicted as a triangle with 100% clay, 100% sand and 100% silt occupying the three corners. Different percentages of each of these constituents give soil its texture. Various textures are shown within the triangle and are given standard names. These are the names we hear about in the literature and aside from the three mentioned above include sandy clay, silty clay, sandy clay loam, clay loam, silty clay loam, loamy sand, sandy loam, loam and silt loam.

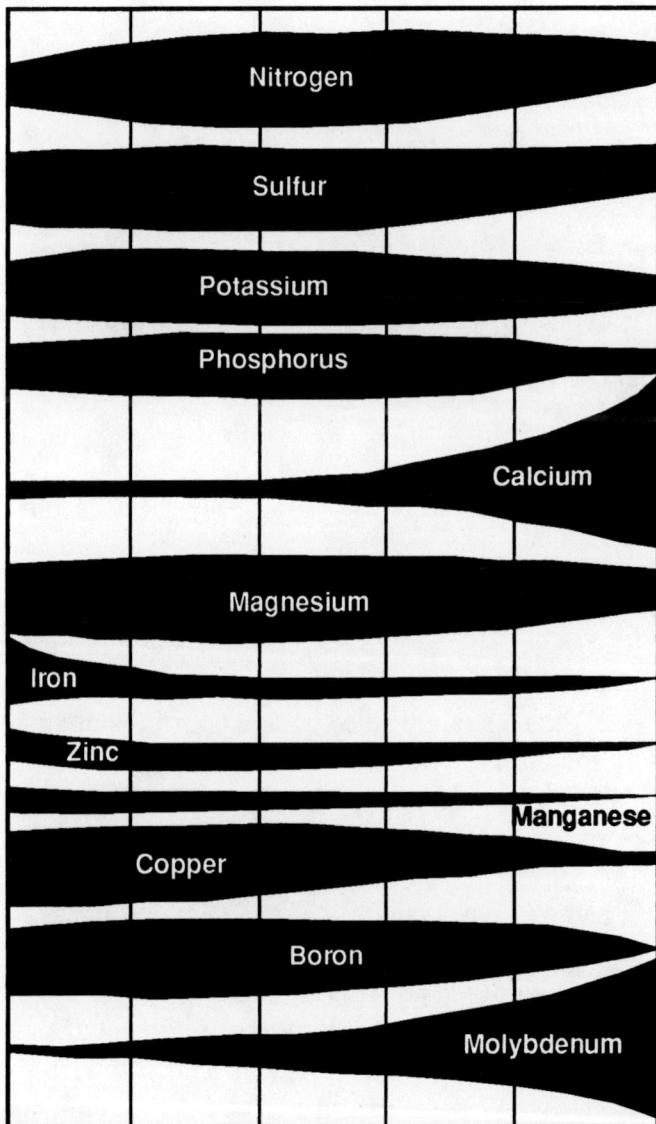

Acid ———————————————— Base

| 5.5 | 6.0 | 6.5 | 7.0 | 7.5 | 8.0 |

Nitrogen

Sulfur

Potassium

Phosphorus

Calcium

Magnesium

Iron

Zinc

Manganese

Copper

Boron

Molybdenum

9

So what are sand, clay and silt? To keep our discussion simple, they are classified by particle size.

PARTICLE NAME	PARTICLE SIZE		
Very Coarse Sand	2.00 - 1.00	mm	diameter *
Coarse Sand	1.00 - 0.50	"	"
Medium Sand	0.50 - 0.25	"	"
Fine Sand	0.25 - 0.10	"	"
Very Fine Sand	0.10 - 0.05	"	"
Silt	0.05 - 0.002	"	"
Clay	below 0.002	"	"

*a mm is 1/25 inch

Soil Type (Texture)	%Sand	%Silt	%Clay
Loamy Sand	85	10	5
Sandy Loam	65	25	10
Loam	45	40	15
Silt Loam	20	60	20
Silty Clay Loam	15	55	30
Clay Loam	28	37	35
Clay	25	30	45

How do I figure out what type soil is in my garden?

1. Air dry a cup of soil from your garden. Remove organics, stones and gravel by forcing it through a wire kitchen strainer.

2. Find a straight sided jar and pour in your strained soil until the jar is at least 1/2 full.

3. Add 1 tablespoon Calgonite (tm) water softener and enough water to fill the jar at least 3/4 full.

4. Cover and shake the jar. Set the jar down and observe.

5. After 40 seconds measure the sediment on the bottom of the jar. This is the sand.

6. After 30 minutes measure the sediment again. Subtract the first measurement. This is the silt.

7. After 12 hours measure a third time. Subtract the 40 second and the 30 minute sediments and this is your clay.

8. Calculate the percentages of each and compare to the Texture Classifications above.

This method will give a rough approximation of your soil texture. Soils with more of the smaller particles tend to drain slowly. Conversely, soils higher in the larger grits drain better. Quite frankly, we don't really need to know the name of our soil's texture, but it is fun to play technician. What we actually need is soil that drains well and we can determine this by simply digging a small hole and filling it with water and watching to see how long it takes for the water to percolate away.

Herbs don't need extremely fertile soil. It is more important to address the question of friability. Good soil texture and proper drainage are achieved through adding soil amendments to achieve the proper soil pH as well as by the inclusion of organic matter.

Organic matter can be anything formerly alive but we stay away from meat scraps and carnivore manures because of potential disease problems. Here is a list of commonly available organic amendments. No Voodoo, just sit down with the Yellow Pages to find all this stuff. There's at least one company in the Valley who will find you whatever you seek.

SOIL BUILDERS

AMENDMENT	N : P : K	COMMENTS
Blood Meal	15 : 1.3 : 0.7	Use sparingly
Dried Blood	12 : 3 : n/a	"
Bone Meal	3 : 23 : n/a	"
Steamed Bone Meal	2 : 30 : n/a	"
Coffee Grounds	2 : 0.36 : n/a	"
Compost	depends on what you rot	Texture improver
Cottonseed Meal	7 : 2 : 1.5	Organic? Maybe
Grass Clippings	1 : n/a : 2	No bermuda
Gypsum	0 : 0 : 0	Lowers pH to around 7.5
Humic, Fulvic, Ulmic Acids	2 : 1 : 2	Adds Fe, S, Ca, Mg, Mn, others
Leaves	<5 varies w/spp.	Acid helper
Manure, Rabbit (hot)	2.4 : 1.4 : 0.6	Use sparingly
*Manure, Horse (cold)	0.7 : 0.3 : 0.6	Caution, salty
Rock Phosphate, Hard	0 : 33 : 0	Both Phosphates also contain
Rock Phosphate, Soft	0 : 22 : 0	Ca, Fe, Na, Mg, B & I
Sawdust	n/a	Use w/ N source
Sulfur	0 : 0 : 0	Lowers pH below 7.5

* Hot and Cold manures refers to the percentage of Nitrogen. Hot is higher in 'N' than is Cold.

Apply the manures and sawdust about two to three inches thick. Apply the other materials 5 pounds per 100 square feet. Till deeply and keep the area moist. There may be lots of other organic additives available to you depending on your circumstances. You might be fortunate enough to know a tree trimmer who will bring you the offal from his chipper or know a chicken rancher (in the literal sense) where you can get the manure before it's been sprayed for flies. Imagination and innovation at work here.

Caveats, Notes, Thoughts

•Manures need to be monitored. If the animals were recently dewormed, the manure will kill all your earthworms. If the animals eat bermuda hay you'll surely get a bumper crop of bermuda.

•Antibiotics in the animals may have deleterious effects on your soil microbes. Some manures can be high in salts and therefore should be used with caution or better yet, composted.

It is important to lower the pH to near neutral because: the clay particles in the soil take on the other, more porous, configuration; the nutrients present in the soil are more readily available (soluble); you will enjoy tolerance among wider spectrum of plants; improved percolation helps to flush Sodium out of soil and to infuse air.

Soil can be acidified by incorporating Gypsum, Sulfur, Organic Acids*, Leaves (especially pine needles), Wood Shavings and Sawdust.

All high carbon organic matter dug into the soil has the temporary effect of robbing what little nitrogen may already be there. This occurs because the bacteria breaking down the organic matter use nitrogen in the process. The nitrogen thus tied up is made available only when the bacteria eventually die. Therefore when significant amounts of non nitrogenous (Cold) organic matter is added to the soil it is common to also add a relatively large amount of some rich nitrogen source such as blood meal. This not only speeds the composting but leaves a surplus of nitrogen allowing you to plant a little early. Everyone next asks "how much do I

* such as humate preparations

12

add?" As I alluded to earlier, I'm a believer in moderation. But the question of soil pH can be best addressed first with the addition of gypsum (calcium sulfate). Gypsum is very difficult to overdose with. I start with about 20 lbs. per 100 square feet of garden worked into the top six or eight inches. Gypsum works fairly quickly at first but continues to be a benefit for two or three years after application. If the soil still isn't acidic enough the experienced gardener will start adding sulfur. Start with five pounds per 100 square feet, again digging it in to the same six or eight inches.

While adding these pH adjusters why not add the compost and other organic matter at this time, too? You should add everything you can lay your hands on. Hay, straw, newspaper, hair from the barbershop floor, compost, sawdust all are good to add to improve the friability and fertility of your soil.

Many of you wonder what it is that we have really added to the soil. Almost everyone is familiar with the cryptic three number designations found on the labels of fertilizer containers. It has probably been conspicuous in its absence that, aside from gypsum and sulfur, we haven't discussed adding chemicals to the soil yet. Well we have added chemicals to the soil.

The three numbers on the fertilizer bag are the percentages of Nitrogen, Phosphorus and Potassium; the famous N:P:K.

But actually there are 16 chemical elements required for plant growth. They and their relative proportions are:

Element	(Symbol)	Percent of plant weight
Carbon	(C)	45%
Hydrogen	(H)	45%
Oxygen	(O)	6%
Nitrogen	(N)	1.5%
Potassium	(K)	1%
Calcium	(Ca)	0.5%
Magnesium	(Mg)	0.2%
Phosphorus	(P)	0.2%
Sulfur	(S)	0.1%
Chlorine	(Cl)	100 ppm
Iron	(Fe)	100 ppm
Manganese	(Mn)	50 ppm
Boron	(B)	20 ppm
Zinc	(Zn)	20 ppm
Copper	(Cu)	6 ppm
Molybdenum	(Mo)	0.1 ppm

What's this ppm jazz?

PPM stands for parts per million. 1 ppm means that there is 1 part of a substance dissolved in a million parts of some solvent. The analogy I like is that of a really dry martini. A 1 ppm martini would have 1 part vermouth in a million parts of gin. To illustrate, it would be 1 jigger of vermouth in a tank truck (about 10,000 gallons) of gin. Gardening is thirsty work in the desert.

Anyway back to the boring stuff, Carbon, Hydrogen and Oxygen compose about 96% of the fresh weight of plant material. After you remove the water, the rest of the 13 elements compose 4% and a most important 4% it is.

Healthy plants require these 16 elements in approximately the proportions shown on preceding page.

Some plants are known to accumulate other elements in their structure but those elements aren't requisite for the plant's health and function. Composted residues along with the nutrients found in our calcium rich soils almost certainly have all these necessary elements.

But what if something is missing? It could happen that either now or later in the season a nutrient becomes depleted or locked up with an improper pH.

There are some very general symptoms of plant deficiencies which can be watched for. However, it must be stated that:

1) symptoms for the same deficiency vary from species to species;

2) many elemental deficiencies display similar symptoms;

3) deficiencies may reduce yields without other symptoms in evidence;

4) symptoms noted may be the result of multiple deficiencies;

5) symptoms noted may be simulated deficiencies caused by other factors like drought, improper pH, flood or other environmental factors;

6) surpluses of some elements may look like symptoms of deficiencies.

Here some things to look for.

Nitrogen - yellowing of entire plant (chlorosis) starting with the older leaves, leggy or spindly growth (etiolation).

Sulfur- mimics Nitrogen deficiency.

Phosphorus - foliage is too dark green or even blue-green. Red purple or brown pigments form in leaves especially along the veins. Reduced growth. Also symptoms of N excess

Potassium-over greening as in Phosphorus with spots of dead tissue (necrosis) on the leaves. Terminal buds may die back. Possibly a N excess.

Calcium - Youngest parts of the plant exhibit die back, blossom end rot of flowers and fruit. Roots grow poorly. Aggravated by a N or K excess. *from E from salts*

Magnesium - Chlorosis along the margins of leaves or in patches or blotches. Other pigments form. Widely varied symptoms from species to species. Exacerbated by K or Ca excess.

Zinc - 'little leaf' and 'rosette' (stunted leaves or stunted stem growth) malformed leaves, necrotic spots, too green or chlorotic depending on the species. Mimics a P or K excess.

Copper - Very variable. From chlorosis to over green leaves with rolled margins. Die back of young shoots with "witch's broom" later. Early death of young plants. Aggravated by N or P excess.

Iron - General chlorosis of young leaves with veins remaining green. May be exacerbated by too much Calcium Carbonate in the soil and overwatering.

Manganese- Very variable. May mimic iron deficiency, also stunted growth or malformed leaves. Possible P or K excess causes these symptoms too.

Chlorine - Shiny, overgreen leaves. Tips of leaves wilt in the heat of the day. You'll never see this deficiency, I just mentioned it to be complete.

Boron - Damage or death of growing tips. Leaves may become hard, dry, brittle, stems rough, dry, cracked, corky. If fruit sets it'll look the same. Poor root growth.

Molybdenum - Similar to manganese. Rolled leaf margins similar to copper. Necrosis of leaf back to the midrib (whiptail). Symptoms more pronounced when nitrate is the N source rather than ammonium.

Add to these symptoms the encounters you may have with bacterial, fungal, nematodal, and other pathogens and insects, the high salt content of our water, improper irrigation techniques, the blazing sun, pockets of nasty soil and a zillion other potential problems, it is a wonder we're not all completely 'round the bend.' ❖

"Salt Burn" margins of leaves necrotic (dead spots). Tips of leaves white with salt. Lack of luster or dull appearance.
Sun Burn necrosis near center of leaves or wilty.

CHAPTER THREE
Planting

Look how far we've come. We have fixed the problems of our soil. And better than that we understand what we've done. At some point we should plant some herbs.

We have at least two growing seasons in the desert. Maybe three if we're careful. For many herbs, the best time to plant is in the Fall. For others it's in the Spring. Either season is worth a shot for any herb in any given year. Be adventurous.

Fall to we desert gardeners is usually sometime in September. This is the season when we can direct sow. That means we can scatter seed right in the row where we wish the plants to grow.

The following year, say in February or March, is our Spring. Spring crops might do well if direct sown but if we encounter an early Summer we may not have sufficient time to establish that all important root system. Therefore many herbies plant transplants in the Spring. Then the only danger is that of the late frost. The frost is easier to deal with than the heat.

Usually around January, we should start some of our seedlings indoors. A sunny window, small table and a couple flats or plug trays full of potting soil are ideal. Ingenuity and/or fluorescent lights can make for up any deficits.

Fill your flats or trays with damp soil and tamp slightly. Plant your seeds at a depth of 2 to 3 times their diameter. Seeds less than or equal to the size of Basil seeds should just be laid on the surface and pressed in, not buried.

Soil from the garden is not suitable for this job in most cases as it contains microbes of various persuasions. These not only produce some pervasive odors but may actually harm your emerging seedlings. You should use prepared potting soil or some other sterile medium.

A spray bottle can be used to mist the soil surface to keep it damp until the seeds germinate. Alternatively, the flat can be covered with plastic wrap and just monitored daily for dampness.

Leave the flat in bright light but not in direct sun. The seeds that need light to germinate will get all they need and the larger ones that are buried are in the dark where they need to be.

If you are using the fluorescent light idea be aware that research has shown that the fancy grow lights are no significant improvement over plain old el cheapo tubes. Incandescents, though, are another matter and the grow light style should be used.

Germination times vary from three weeks or more for parsley to 3 days for some of the easy to grow herbs. Five to 7 days is a good ball park figure.

The first bit of green you see that look like tiny leaves - aren't. They're called cotyledons or seed leaves. The next leaves which grow above are the first true leaves. When these appear it is time to think about transplanting into larger containers. Two or 3 inch pots are commonly used and the rose pots are best because they offer about an additional inch of depth. This helps the roots grow better and also they dry out more slowly and need less frequent watering. Sometimes it is easiest to use a teaspoon to dig up the youngsters when transplanting out of flats. At this stage we need lots of light.

Some plants can get all the way to the first week of March in rose pots and some will need to be "potted up" to a larger size. But either way we should be able to transplant into the garden then or the second week of March without risk of frost. Earlier some years but rarely later. Before transplanting, till the rows once more. Then plant your babies to the same depth they've been growing. Be prepared to protect your new plants from the wind. That is a new experience for them unless you "hardened them off".

It's not unusual for experienced gardeners to turn an electric fan on the baby plants the week or ten days before transplanting to "harden" the tender plants to life outdoors. If you do, start with just a few hours of indirect exposure and slowly increase to direct breezes about half the day.

This will increase water use so be prepared to increase irrigation.

Two problems you may encounter are 'damping off' and "fungus gnats". Damping Off is caused by one of a couple soil fungi which attack the stem of very young seedlings right at the top of the soil. This is most common at the cotyledon stage. It causes the seedling to just fall over. Damping off is caused by contaminated soil. It is better to use sterile technique to prevent onset than to try to cure the problem once established.

Fungus Gnats are small black flying insects. The adult causes small black spots on the leaves which is actually the fungus. This is of little concern. It is the maggot of the gnat in the soil which feeds on the roots and stem of the plant which hurts.

Both problems are encouraged by soil a little too damp. Both can be combatted by spraying a weak solution of Listerine (tm) or a tea made from thyme on the soil surface. In extreme cases of the gnats you can drench (water) with a tea made of tobacco.

Herbs grown in the fall season don't need any supplemental shade. Indeed, the photoperiod (the period of daylight) may be marginally short as it is.

The spring crop, though, enjoys some afternoon shade if it can be arranged, as the days lengthen and the weather warms up into triple digits. However, this is not a hard and fast rule. Many herbs in production gardens get no respite from the intense insolation and, because of a vigorous root system, fare quite well through the blazing summer. They may not grow but they don't die either and they are johnny on the spot for a burst of growth when the season changes back to more temperate conditions of the fall. ❖

© '94 MS

CHAPTER FOUR
Visiting and Kibitzing

Beginning gardeners should try to visit some of the better gardens available both public and private.

There are some generalities one should consider when touring someone else's garden. Our crazy desert growing conditions make growing some plants difficult or seemingly impossible. Yet, some accomplished or lucky gardeners are able to wow us with the flora they've managed to grow.

To emulate and learn from their successes, first, consider the conditions which make plant culture so obviously difficult. Next, try to discover how these conditions have been modified or eliminated.

Sometimes this sleuthing becomes very involved even as the ecology itself is very convoluted.

Remember some of the problems plants have with life in this area are heat, alkaline soil, salty water, drying winds and that kind of stuff.

While we're snooping around do we notice whether an unlikely plant is growing where it will get afternoon shade in the summer? Maybe growing on the East side of a row of corn or sunflowers provides just the edge this plant needs to thrive.

Has the gardener gone to the expense of installing a mist system? Shade cloth? How has she/he changed the soil? Improving the drainage will mitigate a lot of the problems with the salty water.

How is this garden situated relative to the prevailing hot summer winds? I discovered that the most damaging wind at my location comes from the West or Southwest. Planting on the East or North of something large will break the wind. Having a nice organic soil and/or a good thick mulch will retain moisture for the wind blown plants to drink from.

What is the state of maturity of the plant in question? Is it large enough that it was obviously started indoors thus giving it a more substantial root system? Maybe our inventive gardener found a variety which adapts well to harsh conditions.

Whatever the differences between your garden's microclimate and this one, they are discoverable.

There are very few truly new ideas in gardening. There are reorganizations of existing data and there are lucky guesses and there may be hard work or some monetary expense.

If you see an idea that will work for you, Steal It! It doesn't belong to anyone, it's only being borrowed. Just like "our" planet is being borrowed from our heirs.

Whoops, I threw a new term at you a couple paragraphs back. We need to discuss the term "mulch." ❖

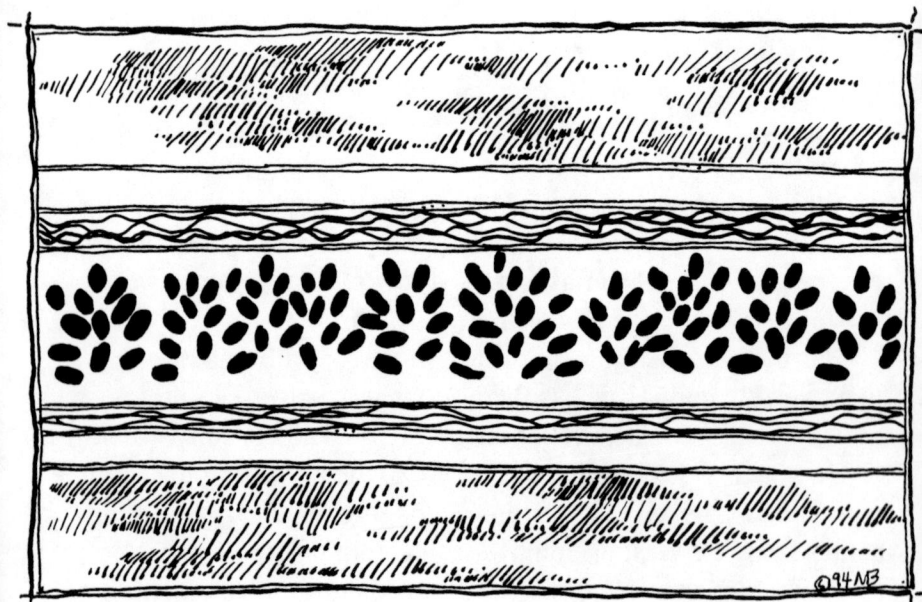

CHAPTER FIVE
Piled Higher and Deeper

Who first decided that ground litter was ugly and had no place in the garden? I like to blame the chemical companies for most dumb ideas. I'll tell why I think they are behind this one, too. Mulches contribute to weed suppression and fertility. These are two of the major arenas of chemical gardening. Naturally they would like to see you use their products to these ends instead of the system which has been used by Nature for the preceding eons with no ill effect.

Our desert home can offer the exception, but take a walk through a healthy temperate zone forest or meadow. What is that between the plants? The soil? Heck no! You see old leaves and other plant offal. That's mulch. Is the natural system suffering from all that nasty mulch? Quite the contrary. Most of us have been taught since we were wee ones that bare soil contributes to erosion. If mulch was bad the natural system would have evolved a remedy.

It's not bad, does that mean that it's good? In almost every case a nice thick mulch will benefit your gardening attempts. The mulch you lay down around your plants shades the soil, stops weed germination and keeps the roots cooler. Aside from a dearth of organic matter in the soil, the main reason we have no earthworms around here is because the soil is too hot. The worms, roots, bacteria and fungi all benefit from mulch. Because the soil is cooler and moister, lots of biochemical reactions aren't inhibited; there's a lot more going on in and on your soil. The water you apply has a chance to percolate down into the soil instead of running off and evaporating. The debate over watering in the evening or early morning becomes less important. The mulch stops that nasty waterproof crust from forming and your water soaks right in.

There are many materials you can use for mulches. Old, moldy hay and straw are favorites because they are easy to handle in the bale, they are cheap and sometimes free, and they mat down after application so they don't blow away in the gales we sometimes get around here. There are reasons to use other mulches. Using wood shavings, saw dust and the like are good mulches when you are trying to acidify the soil (and who isn't?). They don't have to be applied as thick, they will mat down and not blow away. However, they are seldom as cheap as rotten hay. Try to find a supply of manure and wood shavings together. This works really well and the nitrogen from the manure helps break down the wood chips so they can be tilled in the following year with good results.

Grass clippings work well, are free, and add 1% nitrogen and 2% potash. Leaves are good. They rot quickly to nice friable compost. Newspaper, especially if shredded, works just fine and since the advent of soy based inks it introduces no toxins. Rocks, surprisingly enough, work nicely in a perennial garden. They add nothing except shade but on the other hand they don't have to be replaced next season. Manures and compost can be spread on top of them and then watered in with good effect on the plants.

Yes, there can be a downside to mulches. I've had terrible luck using organic mulches when mulching woody perennials until their second years (here's a good application for rocks). They sometimes develop crown rots when they stay too moist. To effectively mulch these kinds of herbs pull your mulch away from their stems at least 6 inches.

How much mulch should you use? Speaking of straw and hay, the late, great Ruth Stout said, "Probably more than you would think." At least 6 inches and maybe 8 inches. This will mat down to two to three inches thick.

Other benefits of mulch are that it keeps your tomatoes and squashes off the soil so they don't get rot spots. Drip lines under the mulch are less apt to be nibbled and pecked by thirsty critters. All in all, there are very few reasons not to mulch unless you just don't like the look of it and I can't refute that. ❖

CHAPTER SIX
Companions Aren't Always Friends...
Herbs helping herbs. Herbs hindering herbs.

The subject of companion planting is fascinating. Unfortunately, very little reproducible research has been performed to quantify and qualify this hypothesis that some plants are benefited by the close proximity of certain other plants.

Then there is the antithesis that some plants are handicapped by the proximity of some plants. There has been some research on this point. It's been found that the breakdown products of ryegrass mulch inhibit seed germination (allelopathy). Also, it has been known for many years that walnuts' roots inhibit sprouting of seeds. The same goes for creosote bush. There are other examples in the literature.

Some people believe there is a god, not because there is any obvious earthly evidence of a kindly and benevolent being "out there" but because there is obvious earthly evil. Their reasoning is that if there is a yin there must be a yang. Therefore, if there is evidence that some plants hamper other plants it should follow that some plants help some other plants.

I will tell you the experiences I've had and let you then draw your own conclusions.

When growing tomatoes I always grow basil in the same row. It has been the experience of at least one reliable source, and good friend, that the Sphinx Moth a.k.a. the Hummingbird Moth won't go near basil plants. Why do we care? The Sphinx Moth is the denizen which lays the egg of the dreaded Tomato Horned Worm Caterpillar.

It was noted that while the tomatoes were the same height as the basil that no caterpillars were present but that as soon as the tomatoes grew taller than the basil the blasted green varmints appeared and wreaked heavy damage. It was further noted that the caterpillar would not work its way lower on the tomato than the top of the adjacent basil plant. Go figure!

One way I utilize some plants as a type of companion plant is as a trap crop. When bell peppers are grown near either mint, catnip, basil or lemon verbena, whitefly will invariably choose to infest the latter species rather than the peppers.

Another way I use companion plants is in the same pot as a plant which is easily overwatered. Plants such as rosemary, sage and lemon verbena which will drown and die in pot culture because I'm a little too enthusiastic with the hose seem to be immune to overwatering if a catnip or one of the mints or a squash or some other water hog is growing in the pot with it.

I recommend that everyone play with all these ideas and when you find a success story, tell two friends. There are some books written on the subject of companion planting. You should read these too but with a grain of salt. ❖

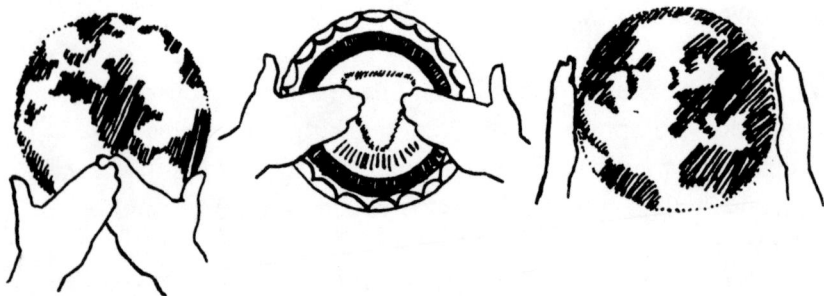

CHAPTER SEVEN
Nein, Herr Komindant, Vee See Nossing, Vee Hear Nossing

It was my intention at this point to tell you about some of the organic pesticides that I use to keep the bad bugs under control on my crops. However, it has come to recent attention that some organic types are running afoul of the law by using harmless concoctions in the battle of the bugs.

One friend of mine, a learned and kindly organic consultant was almost jailed in California for using a common salad ingredient as an effective deterrent against whitefly. I have been using a similar solution for years. It works better than any synthetic you can buy and if you wanted to you could drink it with no more side effect than a mild bellyache.

Another successful organic grower is in deep with the Federal EPA because he uses what amounts to a delicious sounding salsa on his vegetable crops. This is another recipe I'd have let you in on but no way, now. Sorry.

These two fellas each farm or manage thousands of acres. They have been victimized by some really screwy laws written by politicians who are uninformed or misinformed or maybe, just maybe, they've been influenced somehow, and I can't imagine how, by organizations which might be in some, no doubt, obscure way related to the chemical or pharmaceutical industries.

Or maybe they're just unable to write effective legislation.

Can you imagine what the Feds would do to a little (I'm talking acreage, now) guy like me???

Oh! Oh! I'm way up here on the soapbox again.

Anyway, check the bibliography at the end of this tome for some ideas on this subject. I'll let those authors take the heat.

I can, perhaps give you some of the philosophical approaches to organic pest control. You may, then, be able to reconstruct as an independent researcher, some of the recipes I use with some success. If I still get in trouble I'll be counting on all you guys to chip in on my bail.

First, the gardener must learn to recognize the insects which are actually a problem. Some of the ugliest insects are your best friends in this war. I forbid you to use these ideas to eradicate all life in your garden which is just as easy to do organically as it is synthetically.

Next you must determine the threshold of damage you are willing to accept. With some experience you can anticipate the level of infestation which will result in intolerable crop aesthetics.

My pest management scheme involves the encouragement of the vast army of beneficial insects which inhabit the desert. It is well understood in the scientific community that the rise in population of the eater follows the rise in population of the eatee. To illustrate, you won't have an aphid problem until there is fresh, tender, yummy new growth on your rose bushes. Then you won't see very many ladybugs or lacewings until there are lots of aphids to eat.

Similarly, wasps eat caterpillars, so do some of the true bugs. Etc., etc. It is also important to know that the larval stage of some beneficial insects is the one you want to encourage in your garden but to get the larvae you must have the adult at hand to lay the eggs. Many of the adults eat nectar and pollen. They overwinter in weeds and other growth. Consequently you must accept the idea that removing all the weeds will not help you in the long term.

I am not suggesting that all weeds be allowed to remain. For example, I take personally, the affront presented by such bad actors as puncturevine. Another common name for this bad boy is Terror of the Earth. Even the scientific binomial is convincing of its nasty nature; Tribulus terrestris. Though some scientific evidence exists that the seeds may lower blood cholesterol I'd rather eat worms than let this beast live on my property.

If you can not coexist with some weeds, some crop damage and some ugly insects you're in the wrong book. I harbor wasps and spiders in my garden to an extent with which lots of city folks are uncomfortable. I am convinced, though that my bugs know me. So do other visitors to the garden such as the bees. We have reached understandings. We respect each other's jobs and space. I harvest in the cool early morning when the bees are still napping, for example. In all the years I've been gardening as a profession I have been stung once by a wasp. And it was my fault. I carelessly and accidentally attacked their nest with my hedge trimmer. And at that, getting stung only once was a surprise because I was swarmed upon by probably 20 wasps. It was as though they knew I wasn't intentionally threatening their nest but felt they had to warn me off.

If you can, please understand that a little sacrifice is required in order to be organic. By the way, I was stung through my sock. I stopped and cut a piece of Aloe and put it inside my sock against the sting; the pain subsided and the site never did swell up. Ecology at its best.

So, you've found an entomology book and have learned to recognize some of your allies. You have decided that 10% damage is acceptable and that a patch of weeds by the back fence won't send you to hell when you die. You will hate me when I tell you this next bit. That is that if you are just beginning to be organic that you will be infested with hordes of bad bugs for a short while. Some of the most susceptible victims of insecticides both organic and synthetic are the beneficials. Honeybees are like the canary in the mine shaft.

I would recommend that you consider planting two gardens. Plant one expecting to lose everything to the bug burglars. The other one should be the larger of the two and on it use light applications of some organic insecticides to at least get some nice veggies for the kitchen. This is like the sacrifice fly in baseball. You're going to score a run but it won't be a freebie. The sacrificed garden will perhaps get devoured but before the end of the season there will be an amazing population of beneficials. Please be patient this first season. Remember, you get two seasons every year. You will be rewarded. The Grand Canyon wasn't cut in a day. There will be occurrences which will try the patience of saints. One of these is the desert's yearly infestation of whiteflies.

Precepts to organic remedies...

All insects "breathe" through small holes on their abdomens. If you could plug these holes you could suffocate them.

No insect has anything in its "blood" which causes clotting. The slightest nick and they dehydrate (bleed to death).

The larvae of many insects aren't as mobile as the adults and additionally their outer coverings aren't as impervious as the adults' either.

Insects and their larvae are sometimes covered with a coating which helps them keep the water inside their bodies but this coating is soluble.

So it follows that if a person could spray an insect with something that can plug its breathing holes or could cause it to dehydrate, he/she could cause the demise of that insect. If that same person was careful to locate the source of the infesting population and spray only there the rest of the insects in the area would be spared.

Do you remember the horrible pictures of the sea creatures coated with oil dying on the beach after the tanker Valdez ran aground? If an insect somehow got coated with oil it might clog those breathing holes. The same might hold for a plant, which also "breathes" through tiny holes called stomata.

What if there was a way to coat the insect with enough oil to kill it and yet leave the plant unharmed? There is a way to apply a light coat by emulsing a light oil using soap in water. There would be a little oil to plug the holes and a little soap to dissolve the coating on the insect. Then the bug would be impaired and maybe even die. If the oil was a vegetable oil and the soap was a true soap, NOT A DETERGENT, the spray would be harmless to you, your kids, the dog, et al.

If you were to attack whiteflies with such an emulsion it would be best to shoot for the larval stage which lives on the bottom of leaves. You would, in such an instance, spray the bottoms of the leaves. If you did so every three days for three applications the population of whiteflies would go way down. You would never get them all and even if you did, more would fly in but you'd have made a dent and could relax for maybe two weeks when you would have to repeat the spraying.

If I was to make this emulsion I would try about 2 Tbsp. Ivory Snow (tm) or some other true soap, and 1 or 2 tsp. vegetable oil per gallon of water. And I would agitate until there was some suds.

If I had spidermites on my marigolds I would try to physically interrupt their ability to move around and maybe coat the eggs so they couldn't hatch. One thing I might try would be a suspension of 1/2 Cup buttermilk and 1 or 2 Tbsp. of flour in a pint of water and spray the undersides of the leaves where the spidermite webs were. I suspect this would look really ugly on a houseplant and in a day or two I'd take the plant outside and wash it off with a gentle spray from the hose. I'd carefully monitor any plants afflicted for a few days to watch for a recurrence of this tenacious beastie.

After reading some of the books in the bibliography you'll surely have even better ideas than these. ❖

CHAPTER EIGHT
You Always Hurt the One You Love

Let us now assume that you have managed to grow a great crop of herbs. Sooner or later there must come the harvest. Most herbs are what is called in the veggie trade as "cut and come again" type crops. That means that if you harvest carefully and don't kill the plant it will reward you with another crop in a few weeks.

There is some debate as to the proper method of harvesting. Some plants can be cut off almost to the ground and they happily regrow. The chives, lemongrass, garlic greens are good examples.

I recently read a research paper by a range grass specialist who found that fodder grasses grew back faster if they were ravaged down to the roots by cattle than if they were only chewed off half way before the cattle moved on.

The four crops (I'm counting two kinds of chives) just mentioned are not too remotely related to the grasses. Perhaps there is a correlation.

Collective experience with other herbs dictates that not more than 1/3 to 1/4 of the plant be harvested at any one time. This works best in my observation with the woody perennials, the basils and other broad leaved plants.

For the home gardener it's a moot point because the only time she/he is apt to take her/his crop clear down to the ground is at a time when the plants are about to die either from change in the season or after florition.

The 1/4 to 1/3 rule won't ever let you down, the other might.

And talking about herbs flowering, some of them are very tasty. Some aren't.

Basil is one of the latter. It turns bitter when allowed to flower.

Herb flowers are the favorite food of some of the beneficial insects you want to attract to your garden. ❖

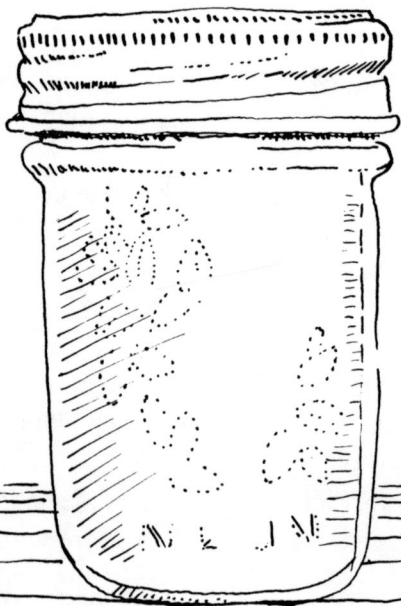

CHAPTER NINE
Save Some for a Rainy Day

I think herbs are best used in the kitchen as a fresh commodity. But in the winter or the heat of the summer we must resign ourselves to using dried herbs.

Herbs you dry yourself are ever so much better than any you've experienced from the grocery store and it is an easy process.

Because we have established ourselves as naturalists we should stay away from the electric powered dehydrators. They work well for fleshy fruits and veggies you might want to dry but are overkill on herbs.

My favorite method uses no added heat. Such a method preserves almost all the intense flavors of your herbs and here is the method I like best.

The herbs you harvested to dry need to be washed and washed again. The wisest lady herbie I know says to wash them until you would be willing to drink the last rinse.

Go to the grocery store and pick up the case bottoms from soda pop or beer cartons. They measure about 11 inches by 16 inches and are about 2 1/2 inches deep. Scatter a modest layer of herbs on one of these case bottoms. If you're very fastidious you can first fit the bottom with a piece of paper towel but I don't think this is necessary.

Place this box on the floor, table or what-have-you. Place another box on top of the one you just filled except turn it 90°. Put some herbs in the second box and add a third box to the stack and turn it 90° to the second box (this means the first and third boxes are oriented in the same direction). You can stack these boxes five or six high. The herbs dry fairly quickly. When they are the consistency of cornflakes store them in airtight jars.

You can pick the leaves off the stem either before or after drying. Herbs with relatively large leaves I pick before. Small leaved herbs, like thyme for example, are easier after they dry. ❖

CHAPTER TEN
Synergies

One of the fun things to try with dried herbs is to make your own herb blends. The following recipes make small quantities and are guides to follow as you customize them to suit your tastes. All ingredients listed are dried.

POULTRY BLEND

1 tsp. powdered sage	1 tsp. marjoram
2 tsp. thyme	1/2 tsp. rosemary
1 tsp. onion powder	2 Tbsp. parsley
1 tsp. garlic powder	1/4 tsp. pepper
2 tsp. savory	

Mix everything together in a blender. Shake well before using.

SEAFOOD BLEND

4 tsp. chives	2 tsp. tarragon
2 Tbsp. parsley	2 tsp. celery leaves
1/4 tsp. white pepper	1/2 tsp. paprika
1 tsp. lemon peel	1/2 tsp. thyme
1/2 tsp. savory	

Mix in blender. Shake before using.

SOUP AND SALAD SPRINKLE

2 Tbsp. tomato flakes	2 Tbsp. bell pepper pieces
2 Tbsp. celery leaves	2 tsp. sesame seeds
1 tsp. mustard powder	1/2 tsp. garlic powder
1/2 tsp. onion powder	

Mix in blender. Shake before using.

MEXICAN BLEND

4 tsp. tomato pieces	4 tsp. bell pepper pieces
2 tsp. celery leaves	1 tsp. onion powder
1 tsp. garlic powder	1/2 tsp. hot pepper flakes
1/2 tsp. cumin	

Mix in blender. Shake before using. Some like more hot pepper and less celery

ITALIAN BLEND

2 Tbsp. parsley	2 tsp. marjoram
2 tsp. thyme	2 tsp. basil
2 tsp. oregano	1 tsp. garlic powder
4 tsp. tomato pieces	

Mix in blender. You know the rest.

❖

CHAPTER ELEVEN
The Essence

I used to worry about the law when I told folks about making cosmetics or health aids from herbs but these recipes are public domain so retribution is unlikely. So how about some other uses for your herbs?

Of course I have to say that I don't suggest that anyone ever attempt to make anything whatsoever from herbs. Especially don't take any money from the pockets of the cosmetic or pharmaceutical companies by using any of these recipes the way our grandparents did. Look what happened to them. One of the ways of using herbs IN THE OLD DAYS, was to make extracts. IN THE OLD DAYS every housewife (domestic engineer) had her still room. The place where she kept the still or distiller.

What are herbal extracts? An extract is a method of removing the essential or active principals from the vegetative portion of herbs. They can be as simple as a cup of tea or as involved as a steam extraction and distillation.

Why make herbal extracts? Many reasons. Extracts allow the preservation of herb essences through the 'off-season'. They allow the concentration of active ingredients as well as the options of diverse types of applications.

How is it done? There are a few major types of extractions. A couple are too dangerous to try in the normal kitchen but most are as safe as cooking lunch.

INFUSIONS- are the same as making tea. Pour boiling water over herbs and allow to steep 8 to 15 minutes.

DECOCTIONS- are commonly used for woody herbs (not an oxymoron). The bark, root, wood, nut, etc. is chopped fine and placed into boiling water and simmered for about 15 minutes, then strained while still hot.

COLD EXTRACT- is a way of maintaining the potency of heat labile components (such as vitamins) in an extract. Herbs at double the amount suggested below are added to the solvent fluid and allowed to steep for 8 to 12 hours.

TINCTURES- are basically infusions, decoctions or cold extracts made using alcohols or vinegar (usually cider).

OILS- are made by dissolving tinctures in suitable oil or as an infusion of the herbs into warm oil.

SYRUPS- are made by adding tinctures to honey or sugar syrup.

OINTMENTS- are made by combining a tincture or oil with bees wax, lanolin, petroleum jelly or the like.

How much do I use? As with many other uses of herbs a considerable amount of initiative is encouraged but some beginning guidelines are to make one pint of a:

Weak extract	1/2 oz. dry	or 1 1/2 handfuls fresh;
Normal extract	1 oz. dry	or 3 handfuls fresh herbs;
Strong extract	2 oz. dried	or 6 handfuls fresh.

What are some uses of herbal extracts? Numerous! Medicinal uses are myriad. In cosmetics they're used in soaps, lotions, oral hygiene, hair and bath preparations. Practitioners of massage and aromatherapy use oils and other extracts routinely. Housekeeping (domestic engineering) uses such as cleaners, polishes, waxes, disinfectants and deodorizers. Dyeing of textiles, yarns, dried florals, etc. There are recipes for making effective insect repellents, too. And the ever popular culinary uses.

Herb vinegars, oils and honeys are extracts. So are coffee and tea and lemonade.

Some herbs used for the skin are:

Elder Flowers- Cleansing, lightening and emollient
Irish Moss- Emollient
Violets- Cleansing, emollient
Marigolds- Cleansing, astringent, healing, toning
Thyme- Disinfectant, toning, refreshing
Chamomile-Cleansing, cooling, anti-inflammatory
Lavender- Antiseptic, stimulating

Herbs used for the hair include:

Blonde- Chamomile, Elder Flowers, Yarrow,
          Mullein Flowers
Dark- Rosemary, Thyme, Sage
Red- Marigold flowers, Calendula flowers
Oily- Peppermint, Lavender
Dry- Marshmallow, Parsley, Elder Flowers, Rosemary

Herbs for oral hygiene are:

Sage- Astringent
Cloves- Antiseptic
Peppermint- Antiseptic
Thyme- Antiseptic
Parsley- Breath
Marjoram- Breath
Juniper Berries- Breath
Strawberries- Plaque

There are so many other uses for herbs that have already been explored to death that I won't bore you with sachets, potpourris, pomanders, teas, swags, vinegars, oils and all the rest.

These topics and many more are covered better in the books that couldn't help you grow the recalcitrant creatures. Some of the ones I like are listed in the bibliography. ❖

CHAPTER TWELVE
The Seed of an Idea

Many sources of herb seed exist. Below are listed only a few of the good ones. There are lots more which you will run into. Some of these companies specialize in a particular type of herb e.g., culinary, dried florals, medicinal, heirloom, etc. Catalog prices, where known are added. Most will refund the price of the catalog with the first order. Many contain some interesting reading.

Abundant Life Seed Foundation
POB 772
Port Townsend WA 98368

Bountiful Gardens
19550 Walker Rd.
Willits CA 95490

Burpee Seed Co.
300 Park Ave
Warminster PA 18991-0001

Companion Plants ($2)
7247 N. Coolville Ridge Rd.
Athens OH 45701

Cooks Garden ($1)
Box 65
Londonderry VT 05148

Earthstar Herb Gardens
POB 1022
Chino Valley AZ 86323

**Fox Hollow Herb &
Heirloom Seed Co**
POB 148
McGrann PA 16236

Le Jardin du Gourmet ($.50)
POB 75
St. Johnsbury Center PA
05863

Native Seeds/S.E.A.R.C.H. ($1)
2509 N. Campbell
Tucson AZ 85719

Shepherd's Garden Seeds ($1)
30 Irene St.
Torrington CT 06790

Richters ($2.50 U.S.)
Goodwood, Ontario
CANADA L0C 1A0

Nichols Garden Nursery
1190 N. Pacific Hwy.
Albany OR 97621-4598

Chili Pepper Emporium
328 San Felipe NW
Albuquerque NM 87104

Herbamed Herb Nursery
PO Box 209
Bermagui South
NSW Australia 2547

The Pepper Gal
PO Box 12534
Rd. Lake Park FL
33403-0534

Deep Diversity
($4...well worth it!)
POB 190
Gila NM 88038

Kitazawa Seed Co.
256 W. Taylor
San Jose CA 95110

Clark's Greenhouse &
 Herbal Country
RR 1 Box 15 B
San Jose IL 62682

Elixir Farm Botanicals ($1)
Elixir Farm
Brixey MO 65618

Roses of Yesterday and Today
803 Browns Valley
Watsonville CA
95076-0398

There really are too many to list but something in the bibliography will steer you toward others. And that ain't no bull.

❖

A good percentage of folks I've talked to don't know about many of the herb magazines available. Some of them are very specialized and some are pretty general. Here are some of the ones I know about.

The American Herb Association Quarterly Newsletter, Kathi Keville, ed. & dir., POB 1673 Nevada City CA 95959. Included with membership in American Herb Assn.

The Business of Herbs, Paula and David Oliver, Rt. 2, Box 246, Shevlin MN 56676. Semi-monthly $20. If you get into the herb business you need this one.

Country Thyme Gazette, Theresa Loe, POB 3090, El Segundo CA 90245. SASE for info. Sample is $3. $17/yr. Quarterly.

Dittany, PO Box 20022, Glen Eden, Aukland, New Zealand. The Journal of the Herb Federation of New Zealand, $30/yr. Monthly.

Focus on Herbs, Kim Fletcher, 5 Coorange Place, Legana, Tasmania, Australia, 7277, $22 AUS. Quarterly. Covers all aspect of herb knowledge.

Foster's Botanical and Herb Reviews, Steven Foster, POB 106, Eureka Springs AR 72632, $8/yr. Quarterly. Foster is best known for his medicinal herbal work.

Garlic News, POB 2410, Sausalito CA 94966-2410, $5 membership

The Herb Companion, 201 E. Fourth St., Loveland CO 80537, A standard in the industry, $21/yr. Semi-monthly.

The Herb Quarterly, POB 548, Boiling Springs PA 17007-0548, good for history buffs, garden design, book reviews. $24/yr. I bet I'd be redundant to tell you it's Quarterly.

The Herb, Spice and Medicinal Plant Digest, Dept. of Plant & Soil Sciences, U of Mass., Amherst, MA 01003. $8/yr. Quarterly

The International Journal of Aromatherapy, 3618 S. Emmons, Rochester Hills MI 48307. Write for subscription price, I don't know it.

Herb Market Reporter, 1305 Vista Dr., Grants Pass OR 97527. Subscription is Jan through Dec. If you subscribe late back issues will be sent along. $8/yr. monthly.

There are more than these, and again, they're in the bibliography.

❖

CHAPTER FOURTEEN
From Spades to Clubs (hearts and diamonds)

For local information on growing and using herbs there's nothing like joining your local herb club. Also, some of the Botanical Gardens and Arboreta are good places to pledge your allegiance.

Naturally, I'll plug my club first.

"The Arizona Herb Association". $17.50/yr. Monthly newsletter, Monthly meeting, Demonstration Garden, Educational Workshops, December bash is not to be missed. Friendly and helpful folks (other than me). POB 63101, Phoenix AZ 85082-3101.

"The Fountain Hills Herb Society". Jane Haynes (one smart herbie), 14209 Calle del Oro, Fountain Hills AZ 85268.

"American Herb Assn". POB 1673, Nevada City CA 95959. $20/yr

"American Herbalists Guild". POB 1683, Soquel CA 95073. For medical herbalists. Write for information.

"Herb Research Foundation". 1007 Pearl St., Ste.200, Boulder CO 80302

"The Herb Society of America". 9019 Kirtland-Chardon Rd., Mentor OH 44060. Membership is by invitation only. Contact Leslie Rascan at the address above for info.

"Native Seeds/S.E.A.R.C.H." 2509 N. Campbell #325, Tucson AZ 85719. Seedhead News. $18/yr. Great for ethnobotanical types.

This is one area where my knowledge is somewhat deficient. To see if there is an herb club in your neck of the desert check the Reference or Reader Service Librarian at your local library, your Urban Gardener at the County Agricultural Extension Office, your local botanical garden or perhaps at one of the nurseries near you or the garden editor in the newspaper.

❖

Some specifics on some individual herbs and culinary accent yummies follow. Any herb can be tried from seed around the middle of September most years. Additionally, some of these can also be grown in the spring from seed but preferably from transplants. Most springs you can get away with planting at the beginning of March. Your individual geography will cause variation.

Perennial plants sometimes benefit from the extra drainage provided by their being planted on a mound. Among these are the rosemaries, lavenders, thymes, French tarragon.

PLANT	LIGHT	pH	H2O	HEIGHT	NOTES
Arrugula	F	5-7.8	damp	18-24"	Fall
Balm, Lemon (Melissa)	S	4.5-7.6	damp	12-18"	Fall/Spring
Basil, Globe	F	4.3-8.2	wet/damp	24"	Soil > 70°F
Basil, Lettuce Leaf	P	4.3-8.2	wet	24"	Soil > 70°F
Basil, Piccollo	F/P	4.3-8.2	wet	12"	Soil > 70°F
Basil, Purple Ruffles	F/P	4.3-8.2	wet	18"	Soil > 70°F
Basil, Sweet	F	4.3-8.2	wet	24"	Soil > 70°F
Calendula	F	5.0-8.1	damp	8-12"	
Chervil	F/P	5.0-8.2	damp	8-12"	Fall
Chives, Garlic (Chinese)	F	5.0-8.2	dry/damp	10"	divisions
Chives, Onion (the usual)	F	5-8.2	damp	10"	divisions
Cilantro, Slow Bolt	F	4.9-8.2	dry/damp	36"	Fall
Cucumber, Pickling	F	6.0-7.5	damp	vine	trellis
Dill	F	4.2-8.2	dry/damp	24-36"	Fall/Spring
Epazote	F	6.5-8.0	dry/damp	18"	Fall/Spring
Fennel	F	4.8-8.2	dry/damp	24"	
Leeks	F	5-7.5	damp	18"	plant in trench
Lemongrass	F	6.8-7.8	damp	24-36"	divisions
Marigolds	P	6-8	damp	8-12"	
Marjoram	F	4.9-8.7	dry/damp	14-18"	cuttings
Mint, Apple	S/P	5.0-7.5	damp	8"	or
Mint, Chocolate	S/P	5.0-7.5	damp	8"	divisions
Mint, Pepper	S/P	5.0-7.5	damp	10-18"	
Mint, Spear	S/P	5.0-7.5	damp	10-18"	

PLANT	LIGHT	pH	H2O	HEIGHT	NOTES
Nasturtiums	F	5-8.1	damp	12"	under 95°F
Oregano, Greek	F	4.9-8.7	dry/damp	4-12"	
Pansies	F/P	5-8	damp	6-8"	Fall
Parsley	F	5.0-8.1	dry/damp	8-12"	
Peppers (hot types)	F	4.9-8.1	damp	24"	extra Phosphorus
Peppers (sweet types)	F/P	4.9-8.2	damp	24"	
Petunias	F/P	5-8	damp	8"	Fall
Rosemary	F	4.9-8.2	dry/damp	to 6'	
Sage	F	4.9-8.2	dry/damp	24-36"	
Savory, Summer	F	6.0-7.8	damp	24"	freezes
Savory, Winter	F	6.0-7.8	damp	10-12"	doesn't freeze
Sorrel	F/P	6.0	damp	18"	heat labile
Tarragon, French	F/P	4.9-7.5	dry/damp	12"	divisions
Tarragon, Mexican	F	6.5-8.0	damp	to 6'	divisions
Tarragon, Russian	F/P	5-7.8	damp		tasteless
Thyme, English	F	4.5-8.0	dry/damp	8-12"	
Thyme, French	F/P	4.5-8.0	dry/damp	8-12"	
Thyme, Lemon	S to P	4.5-8.0	dry/damp	6-8"	
Tomatoes (various)	F/P	5.5-7.5	evenly damp		winter protection
Verbena, Lemon	F	6.0-7.7	damp	to 6'	

Key: F = full sun,
P = part shade (especially in afternoon)
S= full shade
damp = soil squeezed in fist doesn't quite express water
dry/damp = soil is allowed to dry somewhat between waterings

❖

BIBLIOGRAPHY

I have used and enjoyed the following books. They're listed in no particular order.

Buckman, Harry O. & Nyle C. Brady, **THE NATURE AND PROPERTIES OF SOILS,** 1969, McMillan Co. NY,NY

Epstein, Emanuel, **MINERAL NUTRITION OF PLANTS: PRINCIPLES AND PERSPECTIVES,** 1972, John Wiley & Sons, NY, NY

Parnes, Robert, **FERTILE SOIL: A GROWER'S GUIDE TO ORGANIC AND INORGANIC FERTILIZERS,** 1990, AG-Access, Davis, CA

Stefferud, Alfred, ed., **SOIL: THE 1957 YEARBOOK OF AGRICULTURE,** U. S. Dept. of Agriculture, Ezra Taft, Secretary

Coleman, Elliot, **THE NEW ORGANIC GROWER: A MASTER'S MANUAL OF TOOLS AND TECHNIQUES FOR THE HOME AND MARKET GARDENER,** 1989, Chelsea Green, Chelsea VT

Keville, Kathi, **THE ILLUSTRATED HERB ENCYCLOPE-DIA: A COMPLETE CULINARY, COSMETIC, MEDICI-NAL AND ORNAMENTAL GUIDE TO HERBS,** 1991, Mallard Press, NY, NY

Bremness, Lesley, **THE COMPLETE BOOK OF HERBS: A PRACTICAL GUIDE TO GROWING AND USING HERBS,** 1988, Viking/Penguin, Inc. NY, NY

Mabey, Richard, **THE NEW AGE HERBALIST: HOW TO USE HERBS FOR HEALING, NUTRITION, BODY CARE AND RELAXATION,** 1988, Collier Books, NY, NY

Kowalchik, Claire & William H. Hylton, eds., **RODALE'S ILLUSTRATED ENCYCLOPEDIA OF HERBS,** 1987, Rodale Press, Emmaus, PA

Brookbank, George, **DESERT GARDENING FRUITS AND VEGETABLES: THE COMPLETE GUIDE,** 1991, Fisher Books, Tucson, AZ

Klein, Hilary Dole & Adrian M. Wenner, **TINY GAME HUNTING: ENVIRONMENTALLY HEALTHY WAYS TO TRAP AND KILL THE PESTS IN YOUR HOUSE AND GARDEN,** 1991, Bantam Books, NY, NY

Yepsen, Roger B., Jr., ed., **ORGANIC PLANT PROTECTION: A COMPREHENSIVE REFERENCE ON CONTROLLING INSECTS AND DISEASES IN THE GARDEN, ORCHARD AND YARD WITHOUT USING CHEMICALS,** 1977, Rodale Press, Emmaus, PA

Smith, Miranda & Anna Carr, **RODALE'S GARDEN INSECT, DISEASE & WEED IDENTIFICATION GUIDE,** 1988, Rodale Press, Emmaus, PA

Oliver, Paula, **NORTHWIND FARM'S HERB RESOURCE DIRECTORY,** 1992, Northwind Farm Publications, Shevlin, MN

Stout, Ruth & Richard Clemence, **THE RUTH STOUT NO-WORK GARDEN BOOK,** 1973, Bantam Books, NY, NY

and last but certainly not least ...

McRae, Bobbi A., **THE HERB COMPANION WISHBOOK AND RESOURCE GUIDE,** 1992 Interweave Press, Loveland, CO

❖

Notes

Notes

Notes

About the author...

Charlie Humme is a Market Gardener in Peoria, Arizona. He sells herbs, edible flowers and speciality veggies to some of the finer Phoenix area restaurants. His Fresh Touch Gardens is home to about 50 kinds of culinary, medicinal, dye and dry floral herbs as well as to angora goats, chickens, quail and wildlife. He started organic gardening while in high school. He has his degree in botany from Northern Arizona University and recently served on the state's committee which created the guidelines for Arizona's Organic Certification Law.

Charlie well understands the frustrations suffered by gardeners who are newcomers to our desert as he had first gardened in coastal California, Hawaii, the Pacific Northwest and Flagstaff, AZ before arriving in the "Valley of the Sun." A charter member of the Arizona Herb Association. He has helped scores, maybe even hundreds of folks grow herbs.

This book is a partial outgrowth of research which Charlie and others have performed on a grant from the Federal Department of Agriculture to explore the economics of Alternative Agriculture in Arizona.

FRESH TOUCH GARDENS PRESS
8515 West Planada Lane
Peoria, Arizona 85382

ISBN Title Number 0-9643451-0-2